Advent with the Psalms

Paul Galbreath

Art by Tara Taber
Foreword by E. Carson Brisson
Afterword by Cláudio Carvalhaes

Advent with the Psalms
ISBN: Softcover 979-8-895320-19-8
Copyright © 2024 by Paul Galbreath

Parson's Porch Books is an imprint of Parson's Porch *&* Company (PP*&*C) in Cleveland, Tennessee. PP*&*C is a self-funded charity which earns money by publishing books of noted authors, representing all genres. Its face and voice is **David Russell Tullock** (dtullock@parsonsporch.com).

Parson's Porch *&* Company *turns books into bread & milk* by sharing its profits with the poor.

www.parsonsporch.com

Advent with the Psalms

Additional Books by Paul Galbreath

Word & Sacrament: Tracing the Theological Movements of Reformed Worship. Louisville: Westminster John Knox Press, 2024.

Elemental: A Journey through Lent with the Earth. Parson's Porch Books, 2022.

Re-Forming the Liturgy. Eugene: Cascade Books, 2019.

Leading into the World. Lanham, MD: Rowman & Littlefield, 2014.

Leading through the Water. Lanham, MD: Rowman & Littlefield, 2011.

New Proclamation: Year B, 2011-12, Advent through Holy Week (co-author). Minneapolis: Fortress Press, 2011.

Leading from the Table. Lanham, MD: Rowman & Littlefield, 2008.

Doxology and Theology: An Investigation of the Apostles' Creed in Light of Ludwig Wittgenstein. New York: Peter Lang Publications, 2008.

To the Monks at Mepkin Abbey

Contents

Foreword

E. Carson Brisson

Another Advent devotional? An Advent devotional focusing, of all things, primarily on the Psalter?

Yes.

In an age in which 24/7, in a way never before technologically possible, despair, and its children, fear, hate, tyranny, and violence, and their best friend, indifference, seek our attention if not our allegiance, the alternative character of the Advent narrative has never been more needed. Pondering the Incarnation through the timeless voices populating the Psalter has never been more inspiring.

In the pages that follow, Paul Galbreath, Professor Emeritus at Union Presbyterian Seminary, provides a clear and compelling invitation to readers to inhabit the laments and praises of the ancient voices of the Psalter in the liturgical context of Advent, voices that are echoed by the songs of a young, pregnant, unwed, peasant woman named Mary and a skeptical, elderly priest named Zechariah, chosen heralds bearing witness *in* the darkness to the new thing God is doing *about* the darkness.

Galbreath invites his readers on a prayerful journey into the Psalms as a reliable guide on a unique path through the liturgical season of Advent. He takes us on a complex quest, the goal of which is that we be changed, possibly transformed. His intent is nothing less than to bring the Living Words of the Psalter into the Light of the Incarnate Word in and for the world in which we live, in order "to allow the Psalms to open our lives to the beauty and the suffering that surrounds us."

He succeeds.

As Galbreath notes, the power of the Psalms to form and nurture faith, first Jewish and then Christian, is beyond dispute. Calvin characterized the Psalter as providing "an anatomy of the soul" and taught that there was "no more perfect book" to guide the community to and in the praise of God. Teresa of Avila experienced the Psalms' stirring ability to "dilate the heart." Luther described the Psalter as a "Little Bible" and a "manual" for prayer. Augustine saw in them a "mirror" of the breadth and depth of the human condition. Mother Teresa of Calcutta (Kolkata since 2001) asserted that during vicious and prolonged bouts of depression, it was a stitch from Psalm 84:2 *"My heart and my flesh cry out for the living God"* that time and again drew her back from the abyss. St. John Chrysostom spoke of the Psalms as "sacred medicine." Abraham Heschel, who marched with Dr. Martin Luther King, Jr., described the Psalter, especially Psalm 139: 7-18, as communicating to individuals and communities the sense that human life is ultimately vouchsafed by the Psalmist's faith that we are "perceived, apprehended, noted by God. . . ." In the Gospel of Luke, in a passage explored by Galbreath, a pregnant Mary mines the Psalms in her elegant celebration of the God who has looked with favor on the lowly and powerless rather than the high and mighty. The

Jewish biblical scholar Adele Berlin, beyond her impeccable academic work on the Psalms, noted that she belongs to a community that in the praises of the Psalter declares itself guided and sustained by the brave assumption that God is listening (145:18-19), and a community that *at the same time* in the laments of the Psalms faces with unflinchingly honesty the catastrophic possibility that the God who is God, lest divine attention be taken for granted by disregard for the divine will, might find cause to suspend divine listening (22:1-3). Dietrich Bonhoeffer, no stranger to the cost of faithfulness, reminded us with no less than his life and death that in two of the four canonical gospels, Matthew and Mark, Jesus of Nazareth dies, faithfully, with a verse from the Psalms on his lips.

Faith and the Psalms, Galbreath demonstrates convincingly, found each other long ago in the lives of the ancient people who still look in hope, peace, joy, and love to Moses and Sinai. And faith and the Psalms now find themselves anew in the lives of those today who look at the season of Advent to Mary and Bethlehem for those same divine gifts.

After an important introductory word, Part I of this devotional puts forward 27 Psalms and Luke's Magnificat and Benedictus in a format that follows a schedule from the beginning of Advent through Christmas Day. Each scripture lesson is conveniently provided in full (NRSVue), and is followed by a probing exposition in which Galbreath gently assists the reader in holding their own experience up to the lens provided by the words of the selected Psalm. While important historical-critical information is provided when needed, such as sensitive presentations of the meanings of key Hebrew terms, for example *hesed* and *shalom*, the focus in each devotional is on how these ancient words engage, challenge, and nurture contemporary faith, or, more to Galbreath's point and program, how they engage, challenge, and nurture *faithful living*.

The reader will find of particular relevance Galbreath's focus on two central challenges or opportunities for communities of faith today: the call deeply to engage the plight of the marginalized, underrepresented, oppressed, and poor, and how lived faith must address the crisis of Earth's environment, wherein, when natural systems are pushed beyond their rhythms, cycles, and capacities to adapt, it is in fact the poor and marginalized who along with the natural world often experience most painfully the negative consequences.

And there is more. To these two challenges for communities of faith today, Galbreath brings, through the appropriate lens of Advent, a much-needed, fresh theological grounding. Without eschewing the concept of stewardship as a resource for faithful living, Galbreath goes further by explicating a sacramental vision (see his discussion of "holy dirt" for example) of our relationships with others and with the natural world. Galbreath thereby deftly sets aside hierarchical and anthropocentric categories and calls us rather into relationships in a world that is in all its manifestations an interconnected, living, sacred reality. This overarching theological insight is perhaps most aptly, and surely most subtly, communicated by Galbreath's wise decision to introduce each new theme of Advent with a piece of original art that celebrates the four Advent themes through motifs drawn from the natural world. Pausing to ponder each of these drawings, both their distinctive features and their connections to their companion pieces and themes, will delight and inform the careful observer.

Part II of Galbreath's work moves from contemplation to embodiment, from explication to facilitation. In this section, Galbreath suggests important and innovative strategies for connecting Advent reflections through the Psalms with the physical processes of our lives and the life surrounding us. Engaging the Psalms by listening to them as recordings, singing them, and moving out of our regular settings into challenging and inspiring natural surroundings is recommended and described. Galbreath here shares some of his most personal and surprising discoveries of how the Psalms come alive and reach for us outside of traditional worship patterns and spaces. Calvin's understanding of the natural world as a "theater of God's grace" comes to mind. Galbreath's reflections in Part II offer such a rich set of tools for accessing the Psalms in fresh ways, and such a tangible means into the "world" of Part I of his work, that reading Part II prior to following the daily readings of Part I is recommended.

Readers will discover that this "Advent" devotional takes on more than the worthy task of a devotional experience. It is also a theological manual of considerable depth clothed in Advent and the Psalms. It is a book for Advent and beyond Advent, a guide on the journey of faith, hope, and love through which the God of Sinai and Moses, Bethlehem and Mary is making all things new. Galbreath has brought into much-needed, life-giving conjunction the abiding presence of Mary's child, whom she named nothing less than *Emanuel*, God with us, and its life-giving corollary, impeccably expressed in the words of the Psalmist:

Where can I escape from Your Spirit?
Where can I flee from Your presence?

If I ascend to heaven, You are there;
if I descend to Sheol, you are there too.

If I take wing with the dawn
to come to rest on the western horizon,
even there Your right hand will be guiding me,
Your right hand will be holding me fast.

If I say, "Surely the darkness will conceal me,
night will provide me with cover,"
darkness is not dark to You;
night is as light as day;
darkness and light are the same. . . .

How weighty Your thoughts seem to me, O God,
how great their number!

I count them —they exceed the grains of sand;
I end—but I am still with You.

Ps 139: 7-11; 17-18

Introduction

Christians from all denominations share a commitment to the Psalms. Recently, I spent a month on retreat at Mepkin Abby, a Cistercian monastery in South Carolina where I had the opportunity to join the monks in singing the Psalms during the seven offices/services each day. Every two weeks, the monks sing through the entire book of Psalms. The rhythm of life each day follows the soundtrack of the Psalms with its divergent expression of emotions from praise to lament, from anger to joy.

During the Sixteenth Century, John Calvin, the Protestant Reformer, identified the emotional expressiveness of the Psalms as a key ingredient in allowing Scripture to address the full range of emotions in our lives. For Calvin, the Psalms served as a primary source to cultivate Christian piety in the life of the community. This love of the Psalter prompted Calvin to make the singing of the Psalms by the entire congregation central to his reform of worship in the congregations where he served as pastor. Calvin's critics found the practice so controversial that they accused him of filling worship with Genevan jigs.

While the regular singing of the Psalms in worship has diminished among some congregations, other Christian communities continue to work toward recovering the full range of emotions expressed in the Psalms. In these divided and challenging times, the Psalms model the range of raw honesty that many of us feel as we read the newspaper headlines and wrestle with the damaging effects of climate change, global warfare, structural racism, consumer capitalism, and the myriad of other challenges facing contemporary society.

A word of caution is important as we reflect on Christian interpretations of the Psalms. Christians have often mined the Psalms for language that can be connected to our profession of faith that God is made known to us in the incarnation of Jesus Christ. One can see this in the ways in which the Psalms are often used in Christian worship. One can also see this approach in the creation of prayers at the end of each Psalm – a practice developed in the Scottish Presbyterian church that often provides an explicitly Christological interpretation of each Psalm.

Christian devotional practices will inevitably relate texts and experiences to the truth we experience and confess in Jesus Christ. At the same time, it is important for us to acknowledge the primary role of the Psalms in the Jewish tradition and the ways in which they were used in worship. While this set of devotional readings uses the themes of the Advent season as ways to approach the emotional tenor of the Psalter, it avoids overlaying the text with Christological language and images. Instead, the focus is on exploring the range of human emotions that lies at the heart of the Psalter.

A related challenge for Christian devotional readings of the Psalms relates to the tendency to interpret the word "LORD" as a Christological reference due to the early Christian confession that "Jesus is Lord." The result is that Christian readings of texts in the Hebrew Bible often associate Lord language with Christological interpretations. In an attempt to provide a more precise interpretation of the Hebrew text the New Revised Version (Updated Edition), the Hebrew word for the sacred name of God which was not spoken aloud (Yahweh) is translated as LORD (all capitals) to distinguish it from other Hebraic names for God (Adonai or Elohim). While this approach provides a visual differentiation between the Hebrew words for God, it does not address the broader issue that for Christians Lord language is primarily understood in terms of reference to Jesus Christ. In the following reflections, care is taken to interpret references to LORD in ways that are not explicitly Christological. Two additional aspects to this challenge should be acknowledged: 1) Since Christian theology is inherently trinitarian, there will always be Christological association to the readings of the Psalms particularly given the lens of a Christian perspective during the liturgical season of Advent; and 2) Some contemporary Christians avoid any use of Lord language given the hierarchical implications that are unavoidable in the etymology of the English word. There are similar challenges facing the attempt to provide an inclusive language version of the text. While acknowledging these difficulties, I have opted to leave the translation unaltered and focus on ways in which the Psalms can provide us with ways to navigate the emotional challenges that we share in common with this ancient text. The focus on the emotions described in the text that all of us share is one way to underscore the importance of depicting an inclusive vision of faith in the lives of our communities.

The Psalter offers us an emotional road map of authentic expression that encompasses moments of faith and doubt as part of the normative human experience of searching for the presence of the divine in the midst of life with all of its complexities and challenges. I have divided this book into two parts. In Part One, you will find a daily devotional on one of the Psalms. The following reflections on the Psalms provide an initial attempt to point towards the broader possibilities of engaging the Psalms on a regular basis. Each day includes a reading from a Psalm with a brief reflection on ways that the text relates to the traditional Advent themes of hope, peace, love, and joy. While these themes restrict an exploration of the full range of emotions in the Psalms, they do provide examples of ways in which the Psalms avoid simplistic depictions of our emotional states by underscoring the tension that we feel when facing the invitation to cultivate hope, peace, love, and joy in a world where these qualities seem increasingly absent. Part Two begins with an essay on reading the Psalms outside. The prominence of Earth imagery throughout the Psalms invites us to experience the Psalms in new ways when we leave behind the enclosed spaces of our sanctuaries and homes. This essay is followed by a sermon on a Psalm that invites us to name and reflect on our experience of God in nature.

Advent provides an opportunity to practice the skill of reading and reflecting on the Psalms as a way of navigating our intense feelings as we face the blessings and challenges of daily life. Perhaps by acknowledging the complexities of our emotional responses during the season of Advent, we are preparing ourselves for a deeper exploration of all of the ways in which our own lives reflect the feelings of both acceptance and estrangement that we find in the Psalms.

Directions for Using this Book: Since Christmas is set on the fixed date of December 25th, the number of days in the fourth week of Advent varies each year. This book provides the maximum number of devotions that can occur during the last week of Advent. Readers can simply proceed through the readings in the fourth week of Advent and then skip to the readings for Christmas Eve and Christmas Day.

PART ONE:

Advent Devotionals

Psalm 121

¹ I lift up my eyes to the hills—
   from where will my help come?
² My help comes from the LORD,
   who made heaven and earth.

³ He will not let your foot be moved;
   he who keeps you will not slumber.
⁴ He who keeps Israel
   will neither slumber nor sleep.

⁵ The LORD is your keeper;
   the LORD is your shade at your right hand.
⁶ The sun shall not strike you by day
   nor the moon by night.

⁷ The LORD will keep you from all evil;
   he will keep your life.
⁸ The LORD will keep
   your going out and your coming in
   from this time on and forevermore.

Advent 1 - Sunday

Advent begins with an acknowledgment that we cannot save ourselves. The readings for the first Sunday in Advent always take on an eschatological tone; it is a wake-up call that things cannot afford to continue on their current path.

As we begin the countdown to the celebration of Christmas, we face an immediate choice in terms of how to prioritize these coming days. On the one hand, there is a rush of holiday parties and a push towards joining the annual rush of buying and exchanging gifts. In the midst of this frenzy, Advent takes on a countercultural portrait that seems oddly out of synch with the songs, commercials, and frenzy of the surrounding world. What is wrong with the Church? Why is there a reluctance to participate in a time of celebration and a festive atmosphere?

The answer to these questions lies in where we locate the source of our hope. Is it in the approval of our family and friends or in the shiny new thing that we hope to open on Christmas day? The Psalmist points us to raise our vision in order to see God as the basis of all hope. To lift up our eyes from the tinsel and trees and the cards and presents piling up in the corner need not be an attempt to deny their existence. Instead, it represents a way to re-orient our lives to a deeper truth: Our help comes from the LORD who made heaven and earth.

Psalm 42:1-5

^{1} As a deer longs for flowing streams,
    so my soul longs for you, O God.
^{2} My soul thirsts for God,
    for the living God.
When shall I come and behold
    the face of God?
^{3} My tears have been my food
    day and night,
while people say to me continually,
    "Where is your God?"

^{4} These things I remember,
    as I pour out my soul:
how I went with the throng
    and led them in procession to the house of God,
with glad shouts and songs of thanksgiving,
    a multitude keeping festival.
^{5} Why are you cast down, O my soul,
    and why are you disquieted within me?
Hope in God, for I shall again praise him,
my help and my God.

Advent 1 – Monday

We begin this journey through Advent with the light of one small flickering candle. What will sustain our hope in the days ahead? Our Psalm today provides us with two key ingredients: our desire and God's faithfulness. Advent begins with our longing for new life. We carry with us a deep awareness of the ways in which we have constructed our lives that are not sustainable. Our attempts to maintain our illusion of independence and our hunger for success have led us down false paths.

The Psalmist declares his primary desire as discovering God's presence in the world and in his life. As the deer longs for fresh flowing water, so does his soul long for God. His focus is fixed; he cries out in longing and hope to encounter God. He recalls times in the past when he has experienced God's presence. These memories lead him to declare: "Hope in God; for I shall again praise him, my help and my God." Thus, even in times that seem dark and barren the Psalmist finds a way to hold on to hope. This hope is based solely on God's faithfulness.

What is a time in the past when you have been aware of God's presence in your life? How can this memory sustain you in your desire to feel the presence of the divine today? To recall the past is a first step in relying on God's faithfulness to accompany us on this journey through advent.

Psalm 119:41-50

[41] Let your steadfast love come to me, O LORD,
    your salvation according to your promise.
[42] Then I shall have an answer for those who taunt me,
    for I trust in your word.
[43] Do not take the word of truth utterly out of my mouth,
    for my hope is in your ordinances.
[44] I will keep your law continually,
    forever and ever.
[45] I shall walk at liberty,
    for I have sought your precepts.
[46] I will also speak of your decrees before kings
    and shall not be put to shame;
[47] I find my delight in your commandments
    because I love them.
[48] I revere your commandments, which I love,
    and I will meditate on your statutes.

[49] Remember your word to your servant,
    in which you have made me hope.
[50] This is my comfort in my distress,
    that your promise gives me life.

Advent 1 – Tuesday

How will we walk in hope through this Advent season? How can we cultivate a sense of hopefulness that will accompany us on our journey? The Psalmist offers us advice on a way for our hope to take concrete action by focusing on God's teaching. During the Protestant Reformation, John Calvin pointed to this way in speaking about the third and most significant use of the law. The first use of the law was to convict us of sin and the second use was to establish order in our broader communities. The third use was to guide us in God's desire for us to experience wholeness and salvation. Calvin's liturgy even included the singing of the ten commandments following the confession of sin and assurance of pardon as a way to embody a commitment to this vision of life that the congregation shares together.

The Psalmist identifies a way to sustain hope by closely attending to God's teachings revealed in Scripture (*torah*). To meditate and find delight in God's teaching provides on-going nourishment for hope to take root in our lives so that it will begin to grow and flourish. We do not have to maintain this hope on our own. Instead, our hope relies on God's faithfulness and the witness of our community of faith. To remember this word with those around us is to experience hope that comforts us in times of distress.

Psalm 71:1-8

¹ In you, O LORD, I take refuge;
   let me never be put to shame.
² In your righteousness deliver me and rescue me;
   incline your ear to me and save me.
³ Be to me a rock of refuge,
   a strong fortress to save me,
   for you are my rock and my fortress.

⁴ Rescue me, O my God, from the hand of the wicked,
   from the grasp of the unjust and cruel.
⁵ For you, O LORD, are my hope,
   my trust, O LORD, from my youth.
⁶ From my birth I have leaned upon you,
   my protector since my mother's womb.
My praise is continually of you.

⁷ I have been like a portent to many,
   but you are my strong refuge.
⁸ My mouth is filled with your praise
   and with your glory all day long.

Advent 1 - Wednesday

Today the Psalmist invites us to take inventory of our lives in order to recognize God's faithful presence that sustains us each step along the way. In Psalm 71, these memories are bracketed by hope: "You, O LORD, are my hope, my trust, O LORD, from my youth." The Psalmist looks back over his life and recognizes God's presence that has accompanied him from the time of his birth. This practice of reflecting on one's life in order to discern and discover the presence of God offers us a kind of autobiographical spiritual exercise. Where in your life do you sense God's presence that has accompanied you? What times in your life can you identify that provide a basis for hope? Notice that the Psalmist adopts this practice not to avoid or deny his feelings of vulnerability, but in order to address them. To remember God's past presence provides a source for hope particularly in the midst of difficult times. Even when attacked by enemies and surrounded by those who try to disparage and harm him, the Psalmist remains steadfast in his conviction that God will see him through these difficult times: "I will hope continually and will praise you yet more and more."

In the middle of this first week of Advent, we can learn from the Psalmist's practice of surrounding our memories with hope. We can mirror this practice in our lives by taking the time to articulate our hope in God, recall God's faithful presence in our lives, and reaffirm that the grounds of our hope rest in God.

Psalm 78:1-7

¹ Give ear, O my people, to my teaching;
   incline your ears to the words of my mouth.
² I will open my mouth in a parable;
   I will utter dark sayings from of old,
³ things that we have heard and known,
   that our ancestors have told us.
⁴ We will not hide them from their children;
   we will tell to the coming generation
the glorious deeds of the LORD and his might
   and the wonders that he has done.

⁵ He established a decree in Jacob
   and appointed a law in Israel,
which he commanded our ancestors
   to teach to their children,
⁶ that the next generation might know them,
   the children yet unborn,
and rise up and tell them to their children,
⁷ so that they should set their hope in God,
and not forget the works of God,
   but keep his commandments;

Advent 1 – Thursday

A part of the responsibility of maintaining hope is to pass it on to future generations. Just as the first Advent candle can be used to light other candles, so too can our sharing of hope with those around us provide a spark in a world in need of good news. The Psalmist invites us to share our practice of meditating on hope with those around us particularly those who are younger in order that they might learn that from those who carry hope in the form of a tradition that is passed on from generation to generation.

God's faithfulness to those who came before us provides the grounds for our hope. The Psalmist recalls the stories of God's decree in Jacob and the giving of the law to Israel. To share these narratives is to take our place in the stream of witnesses who have maintained hope in spite of the circumstances which they faced. Thus, we find our place between the past and the future. Together we form a chain of remembering God's presence throughout our history. The Psalmist recognizes the way in which our hope in God is linked in these crucial acts of remembering. Hope then is both a way to not forget the works of God and a way to keep God's commandments. May our hope be set on God as we participate in remembering and passing on the stories of God's faithfulness to all generations.

Psalm 146:1-2, 5-10

¹Praise the LORD!
Praise the LORD, O my soul!
²I will praise the LORD as long as I live;
    I will sing praises to my God all my life long.

⁵Happy are those whose help is the God of Jacob,
    whose hope is in the LORD their God,
⁶who made heaven and earth,
    the sea, and all that is in them;
who keeps faith forever;
⁷   who executes justice for the oppressed;
    who gives food to the hungry.

The LORD sets the prisoners free;
⁸   the LORD opens the eyes of the blind.
The LORD lifts up those who are bowed down;
    the LORD loves the righteous.
⁹The LORD watches over the strangers;
    he upholds the orphan and the widow,
    but the way of the wicked he brings to ruin.

¹⁰The LORD will reign forever,
    your God, O Zion, for all generations.
Praise the LORD!

Advent 1 – Friday

Today we are invited to sing praise to God. What can serve as the basis for this act? The Psalmist notes that if our praise of God is linked to those who are in leadership positions, then we will inevitably be disappointed. When our trust is based on other people, then we experience loss when they perish. Instead, the Psalmist invites to us place our hope in God, the creator of heaven and earth. Here, the world around us serves as a source of hope and witness to God's faithfulness. The beauty of nature that surrounds us, from the majestic trees to the crashing waves of the ocean, offers its own testimony to the Creator. We offer our praise to God not as a solo, but as a way to join in the chorus of thanksgiving with all of creation. To participate in this symphony is to discover a source of happiness that is grounded in the One who creates and provides for us and who seeks out those who are hungry and oppressed.

In this portrait of hope, the Psalmist extends our imagination in multiple directions: first, by connecting our praise with creation around us; and second by recognizing our responsibility to care for those who are marginalized. To participate in the liberation of those who are oppressed is to open ourselves to encounter God's presence with all those who are in need. Our hope grows and our praise resounds as we participate in the flourishing of all creation.

Psalm 62:1-2, 5-8, 11-12

[1] For God alone my soul waits in silence;
    from him comes my salvation.
[2] He alone is my rock and my salvation,
    my fortress; I shall never be shaken.

[5] For God alone my soul waits in silence,
    for my hope is from him.
[6] He alone is my rock and my salvation,
    my fortress; I shall not be shaken.
[7] On God rests my deliverance and my honor;
    my mighty rock, my refuge is in God.

[8] Trust in him at all times, O people;
    pour out your heart before him;
    God is a refuge for us.

[11] Once God has spoken;
    twice have I heard this:
that power belongs to God,
[12] and steadfast love belongs to you, O LORD.
For you repay to all
    according to their work.

Advent 1 – Saturday

On this traditional day of rest, the Psalmist sits in silence and waits for his hope to be renewed. At times, it is easy for us to fall into the trap of convincing ourselves of all that is needed in order to remain hopeful. Hope becomes a daunting challenge on our to do list; an insurmountable task that faces long odds in light of the often bleak nature of the headlines in the news. It is precisely at this point that the Psalmist invites us to sit quietly, breathe deeply, and let go of our anxieties.

To wait patiently on God is to adopt a posture of trust in which our feelings of hope shift from our own sense of optimism or pessimism on any given day to a reliance on God as the source of hope. For the Psalmist this image of God provides a place of refuge away from the trouble and travails of daily life. He pictures this safe place as a rock and a fortress that cannot be shaken. It provides an alternative to hope that is based on the accumulation of wealth. Rather than attempt to provide our own basis for hope, the Psalmist points us towards the One whose power is known to us through steadfast love. To accept this unconditional love is to recognize a basis for hope that goes beyond our moods and our feelings of accomplishment. Instead, we sit peacefully in awareness that our hope resides in God's faithfulness to us.

Psalm 29

¹ Ascribe to the LORD, O heavenly beings,
  ascribe to the LORD glory and strength.
² Ascribe to the LORD the glory of his name;
  worship the LORD in holy splendor.

³ The voice of the LORD is over the waters;
  the God of glory thunders, the LORD, over mighty
waters.
⁴ The voice of the LORD is powerful;
  the voice of the LORD is full of majesty.

⁵ The voice of the LORD breaks the cedars;
  the LORD breaks the cedars of Lebanon.
⁶ He makes Lebanon skip like a calf
  and Sirion like a young wild ox.

⁷ The voice of the LORD flashes forth flames of fire.
⁸ The voice of the LORD shakes the wilderness;
  the LORD shakes the wilderness of Kadesh.

⁹ The voice of the LORD causes the oaks to whirl[b]
  and strips the forest bare, and in his temple all say,
"Glory!"

¹⁰ The LORD sits enthroned over the flood;
  the LORD sits enthroned as king forever.
¹¹ May the LORD give strength to his people!
  May the LORD bless his people with peace!

Advent 2 - Sunday

Shalom or peace provides the focus for the second week of Advent. The Psalmist's understanding of peace is envisioned as a state of harmony that descends upon us as a gift from God and permeates our relationships with one another and the world around us. Peace then is not something we accomplish by a series of negotiations to cease our ongoing conflicts, but as a divine blessing that we live into with gratitude.

In today's Psalm, our praise of God includes a request for God to bless us with *shalom*. The movement begins with a recognition of God's majesty. The Psalmist imagines God's presence towering over the grandeur of creation: thundering over the water, hovering over the mighty cedar trees, flashing like flames of fire, resounding and echoing through the wilderness. To recognize God's grandeur is to locate ourselves in relationship to the world around us – as part of creation that relies on God to sustain us. It is from the point of view of our creatureliness that our voices join with those around us in calling out for the gifts of strength and peace.

The pairing of strength and peace may sound unusual to us, but for the Psalmist it points to a collective sharing of life together. Strength serves as a community value in which peace emerges as a central quality in our relationships with God, with one another, and with creation.

Psalm 122

¹ I was glad when they said to me,
    "Let us go to the house of the LORD!"
² Our feet are standing
    within your gates, O Jerusalem.

³ Jerusalem—built as a city
    that is bound firmly together.
⁴ To it the tribes go up,
    the tribes of the LORD,
as was decreed for Israel,
    to give thanks to the name of the LORD.
⁵ For there the thrones for judgment were set up,
    the thrones of the house of David.

⁶ Pray for the peace of Jerusalem:
    "May they prosper who love you.
⁷ Peace be within your walls
    and security within your towers."
⁸ For the sake of my relatives and friends
    I will say, "Peace be within you."
⁹ For the sake of the house of the LORD our God,
    I will seek your good.

Advent 2 – Monday

Talk of peace often sounds like a far-fetched utopian goal. How can we possibly experience peace in a world that is so noisy and filled with conflict? For the Psalmist, peace emerges out of a particular orientation for his life. In Psalm 122, there are two primary foci that establish the locus for peace: Jerusalem and the Psalmist's own home. To point to Jerusalem is to underscore the central role of the temple as the primary manifestation of God's presence with Israel. It is the place of thanksgiving that serves as a visible reminder of God's faithfulness to the children of Israel. The Psalmist notes the way in which the temple continues to bring together the tribes of Israel by uniting them in giving thanks for God's deliverance. Thanksgiving then provides the basis for our petitions for peace; first for peace in Jerusalem, the place where we encounter God's presence, and then to carry this peace within our own homes. The importance of this move is to note that peace grows up not out of our own effort, but out of a collective vision of a way of living in gratitude to God.

The Psalmist then provides a map for us in our desire for peace. While Jerusalem no longer serves as a literal location, it provides us with an image of the place where we come together in community to give thanks for God's goodness. Out of this shared experience, we seek for our homes to become sanctuaries where peacefulness takes root and grows.

Psalm 72:1-8

[1] Give the king your justice, O God,
   and your righteousness to a king's son.
[2] May he judge your people with righteousness
   and your poor with justice.
[3] May the mountains yield prosperity for the people,
   and the hills, in righteousness.
[4] May he defend the cause of the poor of the people,
   give deliverance to the needy,
   and crush the oppressor.

[5] May he live while the sun endures
   and as long as the moon, throughout all generations.
[6] May he be like rain that falls on the mown grass,
   like showers that water the earth.
[7] In his days may righteousness flourish
   and peace abound, until the moon is no more.

[8] May he have dominion from sea to sea
   and from the river to the ends of the earth.

Advent 2 – Tuesday

What resources can we turn to in our pursuit of peace? We have already established a correlation between the place of God's communal presence (for the Psalmist the temple in Jerusalem) and the establishment of peace in our own homes as grounded in the life of thankfulness to God. Psalm 72 provides us with additional clues for ways to construct our lives so that peace emerges within our communities. The Psalmist alludes to three sources for peace to develop. As always, peace primarily comes as a gift from God. The Psalmist portrays a hierarchical linage where God's peace descends upon the king as he pursues the work of justice and righteousness. We can recognize this as a model for our own lives – that the desire for peace is closely linked with our commitment to justice and righteousness. As a second step, the Psalmist locates this particularly in addressing the plight of the poor. To pursue peace then is to address the needs of the most vulnerable in our communities. I cannot attain peace at the expense of my neighbor. Instead, peace is portrayed as the conditions under which all of us can flourish. To seek peace then is to recognize and address the needs of those who are marginalized. We can see this vision of thriving in the natural world. The Psalmist points to the relationship of the sun and the moon, to the rain that falls from the sky so that the earth is nourished in order that "righteousness may flourish and peace abound" (vs. 7).

Psalm 120

[1] In my distress I cry to the LORD,
   that he may answer me:
[2] "Deliver me, O LORD, from lying lips,
   from a deceitful tongue."

[3] What shall be given to you?
   And what more shall be done to you,
   you deceitful tongue?
[4] A warrior's sharp arrows,
   with glowing coals of the broom tree!

[5] Woe is me, that I am an alien in Meshech,
   that I must live among the tents of Kedar.
[6] Too long have I had my dwelling
   among those who hate peace.
[7] I am for peace,
   but when I speak, they are for war.

Advent 2 – Wednesday

Since *shalom*/peace comes as a gift from God, then what is our responsibility for cultivating peace in our lives and homes? In today's reading, the Psalmist calls out to God for deliverance from those around him who are inflicting pain upon him by their slanderous words. The Psalm begins with a petition for deliverance from his enemies before it turns to a confession of the Psalmist's own culpability for accepting an environment filled with hostility. "Too long I had my dwelling among those who hate peace" (vs. 6). Even as the Psalmist declares that he is on the side of peace, he recognizes that he is surrounded by disharmony.

Today then is an opportune time for each of us to take inventory of our environments. Who and what in our lives supports our desire for peace? And who and what stands in opposition to a greater sense of *shalom* taking root in our lives? After taking stock, then we will need to make some difficult choices if we truly want to cultivate an environment of peace. While there are always certain factors beyond our control, we can make choices that create room for peace to flourish. For example, we can choose how to start and end each day. A first step is to take a few minutes each day to center ourselves and breathe deeply, to cry out to God in both thanksgiving and petition, to offer thanksgiving for the gift of each day, to allow hope and peace to find space in our lives. In this way, we take concrete steps for shalom to grow in our lives.

Psalm 4

¹ Answer me when I call, O God of my right!
  You gave me room when I was in distress.
  Be gracious to me, and hear my prayer.

² How long, you people, shall my honor suffer shame?
  How long will you love vain words and seek after lies?
³ But know that the LORD has set apart the faithful for
himself;
  the LORD hears when I call to him.

⁴ When you are disturbed do not sin;
  ponder it on your beds, and be silent.
⁵ Offer right sacrifices,
  and put your trust in the LORD.

⁶ There are many who say, "O that we might see some good!
  Let the light of your face shine on us, O LORD!"
⁷ You have put gladness in my heart
  more than when their grain and wine abound.

⁸ I will both lie down and sleep in peace,
  for you alone, O LORD, make me lie down in safety.

Advent 2 – Thursday

The Psalmist begins his prayer with an acknowledgment of his own anxiety. O God, where are you? Answer me, when I call out to you. How long must we suffer and feel abandoned by you? The starting place for pursuing a state of peace begins with an honest admission of our sense of separation from God and our desire for change in our lives.

Next up comes a distinct shift where the Psalmist offers himself a set of instructions on how to move beyond his sense of malaise. Even in the moments when we feel isolated, discouraged, alone, and depressed, the Psalmist reminds himself and us of a way to move forward. "Know that the LORD has set apart the faithful for himself; the LORD hears when I call to him" (vs. 3). To call to mind God's faithfulness then serves as a way to prompt us in our actions: to avoid sin when we are angry (vs. 4); to reflect on God's goodness and remain silent; to place our trust in God; to lean forward in faith so that gladness finds a space in our hearts (vs. 7). These are the steps that lead us into a peaceful life. All of this leads the Psalmist (and ourselves) to declare: "I will lie down and sleep in peace; for you alone, O LORD, make me lie down in safety" (vs. 8). To pursue peace in our lives is to act in faith and trust God's presence to provide for us.

Psalm 119: 162-168

[162] I rejoice at your word
   like one who finds great spoil.
[163] I hate and abhor falsehood,
   but I love your law.
[164] Seven times a day I praise you
   for your righteous ordinances.
[165] Great peace have those who love your law;
   nothing can make them stumble.
[166] I hope for your salvation, O LORD,
   and I fulfill your commandments.
[167] My soul keeps your decrees;
   I love them exceedingly.
[168] I keep your precepts and decrees,
   for all my ways are before you.

Advent 2 – Friday

Focus. This is the word that carries the day in our pursuit of peace. For the Psalmist, the focus remains on the gift of the *Torah*/the law that provides direction for how we can live in harmony with God, with neighbor, with creation, and with one's self. Thus, the Psalmist declares his intention to focus primarily on the law by praising God seven times each day for the gift of guidance in how to live This is a vision of completeness that provides a direct result: "Great peace have those who love your law" (vs. 165). The search for peace arrives as an outcome of one's focus and dedication on the teachings of God.

As we noted last week (on Tuesday), this vision of life flourishing by attention to the law is one that echoes John Calvin's depiction of the third and primary use of the law as that which guides us into the way of life that is shared together in community. To follow God's precepts and decrees (vs. 168) goes beyond a moral checklist of things to do and things not to do when it develops into a way of understanding the gift of life that comes with creation. Here the choice to follow the law emerges as a way of living our lives before God in openness and dependence upon God's grace. This way of orienting our lives develops as we allow our focus to shift from our obsession with ourselves into a concern for a community that seeks to experience God's liberative justice.

Psalm 85:1-4, 7-13

¹LORD, you were favorable to your land;
   you restored the fortunes of Jacob.
²You forgave the iniquity of your people;
   you pardoned all their sin.
³You withdrew all your wrath; you turned from your hot
anger.

⁴Restore us again, O God of our salvation,
   and put away your indignation toward us.
⁷Show us your steadfast love, O LORD, and grant us your
salvation.

⁸Let me hear what God the LORD will speak,
   for he will speak peace to his people, to his faithful,

   to those who turn to him in their hearts.
⁹Surely his salvation is at hand for those who fear him,
   that his glory may dwell in our land.

¹⁰Steadfast love and faithfulness will meet;
   righteousness and peace will kiss each other.
¹¹Faithfulness will spring up from the ground,
   and righteousness will look down from the sky.
¹²The LORD will give what is good,
   and our land will yield its increase.
¹³Righteousness will go before him
   and will make a path for his steps.

Advent 2 - Saturday

On this traditional day of rest, the Psalmist meditates on the hope of the restoration of *shalom*/peace in his community and life. He begins by acknowledging God's faithfulness in restoring favor and fortune in the past and in forgiving the sins of those who have gone before him. In light of this, he expresses a desire for God to once again bring renewal: "Restore us again, O God of our salvation" (vs. 4). Revive us by showering us with divine love.

When I reflect on these verses, I see the image of wilted plants suddenly receiving new energy as the gift of moisture and nourishment comes over them and prompts health and new growth. "Faithfulness will spring up from the ground, and righteousness will look down from the sky" (vs. 11). New life emerges in the context of relationships. God's steadfast love meets up with faithfulness. Righteousness and peace embrace one another. Faithfulness rises out of the earth and righteousness prompts us to look towards the sky. Together, these virtues cultivate goodness and lead to health, growth, and guidance to move holistically into the future. This vision of *shalom*/peace emerges as we pay close attention to the ways in which our interdependence with God, with one another, and with all of creation prompt us to work in harmony so that all life will flourish. To accept the gift of divine love, to be fully grounded and still open to the sky, and to welcome opportunities to work for justice is to adopt a posture in which peace is restored to our communities, homes, and lives.

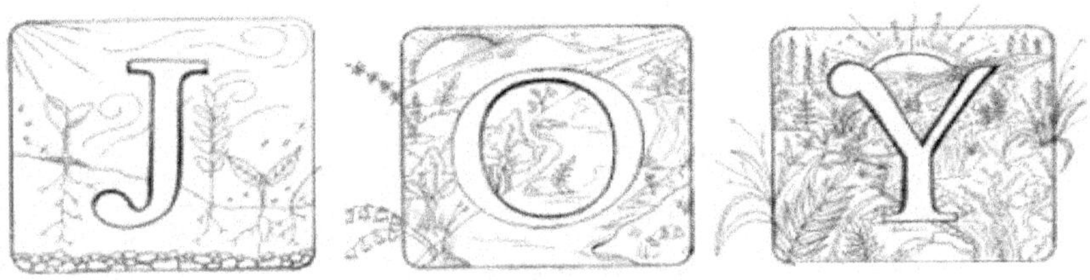

Psalm 100

¹ Make a joyful noise to the LORD, all the earth.
² Serve the LORD with gladness;
    come into his presence with singing.

³ Know that the LORD is God.
    It is he who made us, and we are his;
    we are his people and the sheep of his pasture.

⁴ Enter his gates with thanksgiving
    and his courts with praise.
    Give thanks to him; bless his name.

⁵ For the LORD is good;
    his steadfast love endures forever
    and his faithfulness to all generations.

Advent 3 – Sunday

The tone of Advent takes a dramatic turn as we enter into the third week of this season of preparation. Joy suddenly bursts forth as the primary mood. It is a way to highlight reaching the halfway mark of this season. After the initial wake up calls and the somber warnings about the uncertainty of our present time, this third Sunday of Advent points us in a new direction. It is sometimes called Gaudete Sunday based on the use of the text in Philippians 4:4-5: "Rejoice in the LORD always; again, I will say rejoice."

Today the Psalmist invites us to participate in this grand occasion by making a joyful noise to the LORD. Notice that this is not a solo effort; instead, our voice joins in the chorus of all creation. With the birds and the trees, with the whoosh of the rushing wind and the gurgling of the creek, we take part in the song of joy over the gift of life given us by the Creator. We enter into God's presence with a song of gratitude for the One who made us and sustains us on this journey of life.

Advent welcomes us into the practice of rejoicing; a way of discovering in both good times and difficult moments that God's steadfast love will guide us into the future. To enter God's gates with thanksgiving is to acknowledge our dependence on God as the source of life.

Psalm 126

¹When the LORD restored the fortunes of Zion,
   we were like those who dream.
²Then our mouth was filled with laughter
   and our tongue with shouts of joy;
then it was said among the nations,
   "The LORD has done great things for them."
³The LORD has done great things for us,
   and we rejoiced.

⁴Restore our fortunes, O LORD,
   like the watercourses in the Negeb.
⁵May those who sow in tears
   reap with shouts of joy.
⁶Those who go out weeping,
   bearing the seed for sowing,
shall come home with shouts of joy,
   carrying their sheaves.

Advent 3 - Monday

What does it mean to harvest joy? There's an unusual metaphor in our Psalm today which presents us with a puzzle about the source of joy in our lives. In order to understand it, we need to come to terms with our culture's obsession with happiness. We are constantly barraged with ads and images that link happiness with the values of our consumer culture. If we buy this car, take this trip, wear these cool clothes, then we are promised that we will experience happiness. We often fall prey to the seductive power of these images only to discover the fading effect of these transactions will not last. We quickly wake up and discover that we must come to terms with the source of our restlessness.

In contrast to this perpetual pursuit of happiness, the Psalmist offers us an agricultural snapshot that reminds us that we cannot produce lasting joy on our own terms. A sense of joy grows up in the soil of our lives, is watered by our tears, and ripens under the goodness of the sun. Here the seeds of trust in God sprout in the midst of the travail of life in order to grow to fruition as they are nurtured by the grace of God. Unlike the fleeting nature of happiness, joy springs forth in our lives and takes hold of us. As we see this transformation, our cries of lament turn into songs of joy. It is in this expectation that we join with others in songs of hope: "May those who sow in tears reap with shouts of joy."

Psalm 30:1-5, 10-12

[1] I will extol you, O LORD, for you have drawn me up
    and did not let my foes rejoice over me.
[2] O LORD my God, I cried to you for help,
    and you have healed me.
[3] O LORD, you brought up my soul from Sheol,
    restored me to life from among those gone down to the
Pit.

[4] Sing praises to the LORD, O you his faithful ones,
    and give thanks to his holy name.
[5] For his anger is but for a moment;
    his favor is for a lifetime.
Weeping may linger for the night,
    but joy comes with the morning.

[10] Hear, O LORD, and be gracious to me!
    O LORD, be my helper!

[11] You have turned my mourning into dancing;
    you have taken off my sackcloth
    and clothed me with joy,
[12] so that my soul may praise you and not be silent.
    O LORD my God, I will give thanks to you forever.

Advent 3 - Tuesday

Joy comes to us as one of God's good gifts. This experience of joy is portrayed not as a fleeting emotional moment, but as a deep sense of God's love for us and for all of creation. The Psalmist captures this for us by carefully describing his own experience of moving from mourning to joy. He recalls the occasions when he has called out in grief to God to help him move beyond a sense of despair. Even in the times when his spirits sank into the depths of *Sheol*, he cried out for comfort and relief. This description of joy, then, is not a denial of the pain and loss that we experience in our lives. It is precisely in these moments that our recognition of our dependence on God can turn us towards the source of all life. The Psalmist notes that when he cried out for help, God brought healing to lift him up and experience the gift of joy. As he describes this experience: "Weeping may linger for the night, but joy comes in the morning" (vs. 5). This shift is accompanied by a deep sense of gratitude for God's faithful presence alongside us through the occasions of grief as we allow the Spirit to restore us to a state of joy for the precious gift of life. In acknowledgment of our dependence on God for all of life, we gain a glimpse of the deep interrelationship of all of creation. In this moment, we discover with the Psalmist that God turns our mourning into dancing and clothes us with joy.

Psalm 51:1-12

[1] Have mercy on me, O God, according to your steadfast
love;
     according to your abundant mercy, blot out my
transgressions.
[2] Wash me thoroughly from my iniquity, and cleanse me from
my sin.

[3] For I know my transgressions, and my sin is ever before me.
[4] Against you, you alone, have I sinned and done what is evil
in your sight,
so that you are justified in your sentence and blameless when
you pass judgment.
[5] Indeed, I was born guilty, a sinner when my mother
conceived me.

[6] You desire truth in the inward being;
     therefore teach me wisdom in my secret heart.
[7] Purge me with hyssop, and I shall be clean;
     wash me, and I shall be whiter than snow.
[8] Let me hear joy and gladness;
     let the bones that you have crushed rejoice.
[9] Hide your face from my sins, and blot out all my iniquities.

[10] Create in me a clean heart, O God,
     and put a new and right spirit within me.
[11] Do not cast me away from your presence,
     and do not take your holy spirit from me.
[12] Restore to me the joy of your salvation,
     and sustain in me a willing spirit.

Advent 3 – Wednesday

How does cleansing lead to joy? This is the question that underlies our text today. For the Psalmist, this prayer of confession presupposes the need to make room for joy to emerge in his life. The desire for wholeness and healing leads to a close introspection of his life and a recognition of the need for a new beginning. Taking inventory of one's life becomes a critical step on the path to renewal. Note the process outlined in this Psalm: 1) a longing for God's mercy; 2) an acknowledgment of the need for cleansing; 2) an awareness of one's own failures; 4) an affirmation of trust in God's desire for our wholeness; 5) a sense of hope to move from suffering to joy. This is a portrait of the phoenix rising from the ashes to soar once again into the air.

There is an important lesson for us to learn from this text. While joy comes to us as a gift from God, we must make room in our lives to receive it. Saying yes to joy requires us to clear out the rubble, acknowledge our dependence on God, and lean into hope. The expectation that our crushed bones can become a site where we hear a word of joy and gladness requires a leap of faith. Advent offers us the opportunity to make room for joy in our lives as we turn to God and receive the gift of new life that comes in the midst of our brokenness.

Psalm 98

¹ O sing to the LORD a new song, for he has done
marvelous things.
His right hand and his holy arm have gotten him victory.
² The LORD has made known his victory;
    he has revealed his vindication in the sight of the nations.
³ He has remembered his steadfast love and faithfulness
    to the house of Israel.
All the ends of the earth have seen the victory of our God.

⁴ Make a joyful noise to the LORD, all the earth;
    break forth into joyous song and sing praises.
⁵ Sing praises to the LORD with the lyre,
    with the lyre and the sound of melody.
⁶ With trumpets and the sound of the horn
    make a joyful noise before the King, the LORD.

⁷ Let the sea roar and all that fills it,
    the world and those who live in it.
⁸ Let the floods clap their hands;
    let the hills sing together for joy
⁹ at the presence of the LORD, for he is coming
    to judge the earth.
He will judge the world with righteousness
    and the peoples with equity.

Advent 3 - Thursday

How are you feeling today? It is a common question that we ask ourselves and those around us. It offers us a way to look at our lives and gauge our emotional and physical states. While it is important to be aware of our sense of well-being and to be sensitive to the conditions of those around us, we can read today's Psalm as an alternative way to locate ourselves in a state of joy. Rather than starting from our feelings perhaps we can begin by rehearsing the rationale for us to anticipate and experience joy in our lives in spite of the circumstances in which we find ourselves on any given day.

To sing a new song to the LORD is to allow our lives to be shaped by praise. To make a joyful noise and to break out in a joyful song is to practice ways that joy will guide us through the day. Here we see the significance of anticipating how our lives can be shaped by joy. The Psalmist notes that this joyful song is not an act of self-deception or done in isolation. Instead, the song of joy emerges out of the deep, shared memory of God's steadfast love and faithfulness to us. Likewise, our song joins the chorus of all creation in praise to God. Life-giving water provides the percussive accompaniment with the sea roaring and the floods clapping their hands. The earth itself joins in this song of joy in hope of God's coming in righteousness.

Psalm 118:24-30

[24] This is the day that the LORD has made;
    let us rejoice and be glad in it.
[25] Save us, we beseech you, O LORD!
    O LORD, we beseech you, give us success!

[26] Blessed is the one who comes in the name of the LORD.
    We bless you from the house of the LORD.
[27] The LORD is God,
    and he has given us light.
Bind the festal procession with branches,
    up to the horns of the altar.

[28] You are my God, and I will give thanks to you;
    you are my God; I will extol you.

[29] O give thanks to the LORD, for he is good,
    for his steadfast love endures forever.

Advent 3 - Friday

In a world full of negative news and toxic headlines, why should we rejoice? Today's Psalm reminds us that our reason for joy grows out of a deep belief that God creates each day and that it comes to us as a gift. From this perspective, the reason for joy is not connected to our surroundings, our mood, or our particular predicament. Even in the midst of trouble and in a world filled with problems, we receive the gift of a new day with all of its possibilities as a gift from God. The Psalmist begins with this recognition and then turns to a prayer of supplication. First joy, then a plea for God to save us. Joy provides the ground from which our cry for help rises up to heaven.

When we perceive and experience each day as a gift from God and as a reason for joy, then we prepare ourselves to respond to all that may come our way. Joy is not a denial of the real issues that each of us faces. Instead, it is a starting place to ask for God's continued presence in anticipation and hope. We look to those around us as messengers of God who bring us blessings. We give thanks to God whose steadfast love endures forever. Joy is a posture that we take in hope and faith that we will move through this day with all of its challenges accompanied by the Spirit's presence.

Psalm 63:1-7

[1] O God, you are my God; I seek you;
  my soul thirsts for you;
my flesh faints for you,
  as in a dry and weary land where there is no water.
[2] So I have looked upon you in the sanctuary,
  beholding your power and glory.
[3] Because your steadfast love is better than life,
  my lips will praise you.
[4] So I will bless you as long as I live;
  I will lift up my hands and call on your name.

[5] My soul is satisfied as with a rich feast,
  and my mouth praises you with joyful lips
[6] when I think of you on my bed
  and meditate on you in the watches of the night,
[7] for you have been my help,
  and in the shadow of your wings I sing for joy.

Advent 3 - Saturday

Resting in joy is the theme of today's Psalm. The Psalmist describes the way in which he orients his life in order to allow joy to guide him on his journey. To know that God's resting place is in the sanctuary provides the Psalmist with a place to go in times of need. While one can think of this text in the literal terms of David going to the temple as a place to encounter the presence of God, we can also read it in terms of prompting ourselves to reflect on the sacred places of our own lives. Where do we go to experience the presence of the divine? Where does God's power and glory overwhelm us and prompt us to raise our hands in praise? Like David, when we identify times and places where we have experienced God's presence then we discover resources that will help us recognize God's faithfulness that sustain us on our journey through life.

Just as the Psalmist pictures God's resting place in the sanctuary, we too can develop places of rest that provide us with relief during times of turmoil. The gift of sabbath days provides us with a chance to revisit the places in which we can dwell in God's presence and grow into the practice of trusting that God provides for us. In these moments, we join in the song of praise in which we proclaim that our souls are satisfied. To rest in joy is to let go of our frantic pursuit of that which is new in order to meditate on that which truly gives us life.

Psalm 36:5-10

⁵ Your steadfast love, O LORD, extends to the heavens,
  your faithfulness to the clouds.
⁶ Your righteousness is like the mighty mountains;
  your judgments are like the great deep;
  you save humans and animals alike, O LORD.

⁷ How precious is your steadfast love, O God!
  All people may take refuge in the shadow of your wings.
⁸ They feast on the abundance of your house,
  and you give them drink from the river of your delights.
⁹ For with you is the fountain of life;
  in your light we see light.

¹⁰ O continue your steadfast love to those who know you
  and your salvation to the upright of heart!

Advent 4 - Sunday

In the Psalms, one of the prominent words for love is *hesed* which is often translated as loving kindness or steadfast love. Rather than focus on love as a romantic, emotional feeling, this understanding of love emphasizes a sense of dedication and action to the object of one's love. Our Psalm for today provides a helpful orientation to the relational nature of *hesed*/love. God provides the model of these relationships since all life comes from and depends on God for its existence. God's steadfast love reaches out to hold the universe in place from the heavens and the clouds to the mountains and the great deep. In this portrait, creation is held in place by divine love. Within this greater context, we experience the salvation of human and animals as the loving work of God who longs for the flourishing of all creation.

A steadfast love as that which connects all life is a stark contrast to love that is focused on our human desire and personal fulfillment. The Psalmist points us to an understanding of love that moves beyond our individual obsession and grounds us in a vision of the deep interconnection of life where salvation correlates with the wholeness of all life. This perspective prompts the Psalmist to proclaim how precious God's love is since it provides a place of refuge for all people. Divine love as the fountain of life brings us nourishment and guides us in the way to live.

Psalm 103:8-18

⁸ The LORD is merciful and gracious,
    slow to anger and abounding in steadfast love.
⁹ He will not always accuse, nor will he keep his anger
forever.
¹⁰ He does not deal with us according to our sins
    nor repay us according to our iniquities.
¹¹ For as the heavens are high above the earth,
    so great is his steadfast love toward those who fear him;
¹² as far as the east is from the west,
    so far he removes our transgressions from us.
¹³ As a father has compassion for his children,
    so the LORD has compassion for those who fear him.
¹⁴ For he knows how we were made;
    he remembers that we are dust.

¹⁵ As for mortals, their days are like grass;
    they flourish like a flower of the field;
¹⁶ for the wind passes over it, and it is gone,
    and its place knows it no more.
¹⁷ But the steadfast love of the LORD is from everlasting to
everlasting
    on those who fear him, and his righteousness to
children's children,
¹⁸ to those who keep his covenant
    and remember to do his commandments.

Advent 4 - Monday

As the song goes: love is in the air. While the Psalmist is more specific in terms of God as the source of this love, nevertheless he shares the sense of the song lyrics that love is in the whisper of the trees and the thunder of the sea since for the Psalmist love is woven into the fabric of the universe. In Psalm 103, we can trace the movement of God's lovingkindness (*hesed*) that is extended to us in spite of our sin. The immensity of this love cannot be contained even in the vast expanse of the universe – beyond the heights of the heavens or the distance between east and west. It is the love of One who created us out of the dust of the earth. This love is guided by compassion that longs for humans to flourish by joining in the song of love that guides all creation.

Divine love remains the only source of permanence. As humans, we wrestle with our frailty and finitude. We are here and then we will be gone. Our days are numbered. Yet in the midst of this constant change the steadfast love of God continues. To acknowledge our dependence on God is to align ourselves with love and to receive the gift of God's teachings known to us in the commandments and shown to us in the covenant promises embodied in communities of faith. The Psalmist invites us to experience the mystery through which steadfast love provides us with a soundtrack for our lives.

Psalm 92:1-5, 12-15

[1] It is good to give thanks to the LORD,
  to sing praises to your name, O Most High,
[2] to declare your steadfast love in the morning
  and your faithfulness by night,
[3] to the music of the lute and the harp,
  to the melody of the lyre.
[4] For you, O LORD, have made me glad by your work;
  at the works of your hands I sing for joy.

[5] How great are your works, O LORD!
  Your thoughts are very deep!
[12] The righteous flourish like the palm tree
  and grow like a cedar in Lebanon.
[13] They are planted in the house of the LORD;
  they flourish in the courts of our God.
[14] In old age they still produce fruit;
  they are always green and full of sap,
[15] showing that the LORD is upright;
  he is my rock, and there is no unrighteousness in him.

Advent 4 - Tuesday

It can be tempting to speak of love in generic terms as a kind of sentimental feeling that can prop us up when we are feeling low. The Psalmist offers us a more specific vision for ways in which love can undergird our lives. To start the day with thanksgiving for God's steadfast love is to make room for the divine love song to take shape in our lives. What does it look like to declare God's lovingkindness in the morning? One way of reflecting on this recommendation is through the approach of Ignatius of Loyola. Ignatian spirituality invites us to take inventory of our lives by asking ourselves where we have experienced God's presence in our lives each day as well as where we anticipate encountering God. Notice the way that this approach provides a parallel to the depiction in the Psalm of declaring God's love in the morning and God's faithfulness at night. This work involves an active remembering of the times and places where we recognize God's presence that makes us glad and brings us joy.

Love is the basis for thanksgiving to become a daily practice in our lives. It is good to give thanks to God each day because God's lovingkindness sustains us. As we grow into the daily practice of expressing gratitude for the grace that sustains our lives, we discover the way in which divine love guides us. By adopting these practices, we flourish like the trees around us that grow and produce an abundance of fruit that provides a bountiful harvest.

Psalm 143:1-8

¹ Hear my prayer, O LORD;
    give ear to my supplications in your faithfulness;
    answer me in your righteousness.
² Do not enter into judgment with your servant,
    for no one living is righteous before you.

³ For the enemy has pursued me, crushing my life to the ground,
    making me sit in darkness like those long dead.
⁴ Therefore my spirit faints within me;
    my heart within me is appalled.

⁵ I remember the days of old; I think about all your deeds;
    I meditate on the works of your hands.
⁶ I stretch out my hands to you;
    my soul thirsts for you like a parched land.

⁷ Answer me quickly, O LORD; my spirit fails.
Do not hide your face from me,
    or I shall be like those who go down to the Pit.
⁸ Let me hear of your steadfast love in the morning,
    for in you I put my trust.
Teach me the way I should go,
    for to you I lift up my soul.

Advent 4 - Wednesday

Psalm 143 is a prayer of deliverance where the Psalmist calls out for God to save him from those who seek to do harm. In the context of fear, the Psalmist offers us a way to respond when we share a sense of anxiety that we are experiencing oppression. The first step is to call out to God to hear and respond to us. For the Psalmist, this plea is based not upon his own sense of righteousness but solely on God's faithfulness. As a source of encouragement, the Psalmist recalls times of trouble in the past when God has delivered him from the hands of his enemies. To remember the days of old (vs. 5) is to prod ourselves into believing that God will deliver us. In faith, we too stretch out our hands to God in hope we will hear again of God's lovingkindness. The Psalmist serves as a witness to us of God's faithfulness to us. In a similar way, the words of encouragement that we offer to one another provide a testimony to the liberation we have received from God in previous times.

Twice in this Psalm we read the request for God to teach us the way to move forward so that we may align our lives with the divine hope for all of creation to flourish. We can join with the Psalmist in calling on the Spirit to lead us on the path of righteousness so that steadfast love will preserve us from all harm.

Psalm 138

¹ I give you thanks, O LORD, with my whole heart;
    before the gods I sing your praise;
² I bow down toward your holy temple
    and give thanks to your name for your steadfast love and
your faithfulness,
    for you have exalted your name and your word
    above everything.
³ On the day I called, you answered me;
    you increased my strength of soul.

⁴ All the kings of the earth shall praise you, O LORD,
    for they have heard the words of your mouth.
⁵ They shall sing of the ways of the LORD,
    for great is the glory of the LORD.
⁶ For though the LORD is high, he regards the lowly,
    but the haughty he perceives from far away.

⁷ Though I walk in the midst of trouble,
    you preserve me against the wrath of my enemies;
you stretch out your hand,
    and your right hand delivers me.
⁸ The LORD will fulfill his purpose for me;
    your steadfast love, O LORD, endures forever.
    Do not forsake the work of your hands.

Advent 4 - Thursday

Thanksgiving takes shape in our bodies. The Psalmist invites us to offer our gratitude to God with our whole hearts by bowing down and acknowledging God's lovingkindness and faithfulness that sustain us on our journey through life as we receive the strength for each day. Practicing this posture of gratitude on a regular basis instills in us the habit of living gratefully. This ritual of daily giving thanks for God's blessings provides us with a resource that can guide us through turbulent times so that we can join the Psalmist in acknowledging that when we find ourselves in perilous moments God will preserve us and reach out and deliver us. Notice how our meditation on the Psalms provides us with a pattern for developing a daily pattern of offering thanks and praise for God's steadfast love.

The Psalmist notes the foundational basis of God's steadfast love in delivering us from times of trouble. No matter what challenges we face, love is the source through which God's purpose is fulfilled in our lives. While our circumstances in life change from day to day, God's love endures forever.

Psalm 40:1-11

[1] I waited patiently for the LORD; he inclined to me and heard my cry. [2] He drew me up from the desolate pit, out of the miry bog, and set my feet upon a rock, making my steps secure. [3] He put a new song in my mouth, a song of praise to our God. Many will see and fear and put their trust in the LORD.

[4] Happy are those who make the LORD their trust,   who do not turn to the proud, to those who go astray after false gods.
[5] You have multiplied, O LORD my God, your wondrous deeds and your thoughts toward us; none   can compare with you.
Were I to proclaim and tell of them, they would be more than can be counted.

[6] Sacrifice and offering you do not desire, but you have given me an open ear.
Burnt offering and sin offering you have not required.
[7] Then I said, "Here I am; in the scroll of the book it is written of me.
[8] I delight to do your will, O my God; your law is within my heart."

[9] I have told the glad news of deliverance in the great congregation;
    see, I have not restrained my lips, as you know,
O LORD.

[10] I have not hidden your saving help within my heart;
    I have spoken of your faithfulness and your salvation;
I have not concealed your steadfast love and your
faithfulness from the great congregation.

[11] Do not, O LORD, withhold your mercy from me;
let your steadfast love and your faithfulness keep me safe
forever.

Advent 4 - Friday

The Psalmist offers us a vision of God's steadfast love as a primary way to recognize our mutual dependence on God and the interrelationship of all life. This vision of divine love that is woven through creation provides us with a unitive perspective in which we recognize the way in which all life relies on the goodness of the creator. How will we respond to a vision of steadfast love which recognizes that our interdependence and connection with all life is grounded in the gracious presence of God? Psalm 40 suggests that thanksgiving for divine love becomes the primary soundtrack for our lives. This song of gratitude bubbles up from within us and breaks forth into praise that God delivers us from despair and desolation. Notice that even the song itself comes as God's gift. It is God who puts a new sound in our mouths. Our happiness grows out of placing our trust in God's presence known to us in the steadfast love that heals creation. This is the good news of deliverance that prompts us to speak of God's steadfast love and faithfulness.

This song of gratitude also resonates as a petition for God's ongoing presence in our lives. May God's mercy and steadfast love provide us with safety and harbor us from all evil. Love recognizes and names the existential threat of suffering and evil but refuses to yield to a sense of nihilism. Our experience of God's faithfulness in the past provides a basis for us to anticipate and experience that steadfast love will guide us into the future.

The Magnificat: Luke 1:46-55

[46] "My soul magnifies the LORD,
[47] and my spirit rejoices in God my Savior,
[48] for he has looked with favor on the lowly state of his servant.
  Surely from now on all generations will call me blessed,
[49] for the Mighty One has done great things for me,
  and holy is his name;
[50] indeed, his mercy is for those who fear him
  from generation to generation.
[51] He has shown strength with his arm;
  he has scattered the proud in the imagination of their hearts.
[52] He has brought down the powerful from their thrones
  and lifted up the lowly;
[53] he has filled the hungry with good things
  and sent the rich away empty.
[54] He has come to the aid of his child Israel,
  in remembrance of his mercy,
[55] according to the promise he made to our ancestors,
  to Abraham and to his descendants forever."

Christmas Eve

The Song of Mary provides a model of faithful response to God's unexpected presence in our lives. For Mary, this comes in the midst of her uncertainty about her future. Mary seeks to take in the news from the angel Gabriel that she is pregnant and that her child comes as a special blessing from God. She hurries to the house of her cousin Elizabeth in hopes that this older woman can help her sort through the changes that her body is experiencing. Elizabeth immediately senses this as a sacred moment and offers a blessing to Mary and her child. For Mary, these words of affirmation prompt her to break forth in a song of thanksgiving as she offers herself, body and soul, to God.

At the center of Mary's song is a deep recognition that God moves in unexpected ways and places. God dismisses those who are proud and brings down the powerful. God lifts up the lowly and fills the hungry with good things. On Christmas eve, the message of the Magnificat provides us with an important insight on how to align our lives with God's liberative work in the world. Mary's song invites us to leave behind our expectations of power and privilege that far too often create a vision of the divine that coincides with our own interests. Instead, Mary reminds us that whenever we befriend those who are marginalized, we gain the opportunity to see God at work bringing new life into the world.

The Benedictus: Luke 1:68-79

[68] "Blessed be the LORD God of Israel,
    for he has looked favorably on his people and redeemed
them.
[69] He has raised up a mighty savior for us
    in the house of his child David,
[70] as he spoke through the mouth of his holy prophets from
of old,
[71] that we would be saved from our enemies and from the
hand of all who hate us.
[72] Thus he has shown the mercy promised to our ancestors
    and has remembered his holy covenant,
[73] the oath that he swore to our ancestor Abraham,
to grant us [74] that we, being rescued from the hands of our
enemies,
might serve him without fear, [75] in holiness and
righteousness
    in his presence all our days.
[76] And you, child, will be called the prophet of the Most
High,
    for you will go before the LORD to prepare his ways,
[77] to give his people knowledge of salvation
    by the forgiveness of their sins.
[78] Because of the tender mercy of our God,
    the dawn from on high will break upon us,
[79] to shine upon those who sit in darkness and in the shadow
of death,
    to guide our feet into the way of peace."

Christmas Day

The song of Zechariah provides us with a final pattern of praise and thanksgiving on our journey from Advent to Christmas day. Zechariah (Elizabeth's spouse) joins in the celebration of good news both at the birth of his own son, John the Baptist, but also in anticipation of the birth of Jesus by Mary. Zechariah's canticle takes the form of prophecy regarding God's redemptive action in the world. It begins with praise to God who looks favorably on us and works for our liberation. Zechariah recalls the words of the prophets who have promised God's salvation going all the way back to God's covenant with Abraham.

Zechariah points to the birth of his son, John, as a continuing sign of God's commitment to bring salvation. John will prepare the way for the coming of the messiah, God's anointed one. In keeping with the prophetic witness, John will bring knowledge of God's salvation through the forgiveness of sins. With the help of the Song of Zechariah, we continue to celebrate this good news that in Jesus Christ the good news of the Gospel is made known to us. In the birth of Jesus, the light of the world shines upon us and will guide our path in the way of peace. Today hope, peace, joy, and love come together in the story of a baby who lies in the manger. With the angels let us sing: "Glory to God in the highest heaven and on earth peace among those whom he favors" (Luke 2:14).

PART TWO:

Earth and the Psalms

Taking the Psalms Outside

I started out with a simple idea: at the beginning of Advent, I began reading the book of Psalms outside. My decision grew out of a growing interest in the language of nature that is replete throughout the Psalter. For a long time, I have been intrigued by the ways in which our physical surroundings effect the ways in which we read and interpret texts. Several years ago, I wrote a lectionary commentary while primarily working from the Multnomah County public library in downtown Portland, Oregon. I quickly noticed how my reading of biblical texts on the poor intersected with my encounters with the myriad of homeless people who surrounded me in the library. This experience led me to develop an assignment for my theology class where I asked students to read Acts 17:16-34 (Paul's sermon in Athens) in three different locations and note the different ways in which they interpreted the text. The first time I tried this with a class I was astounded by a report from an African American woman who described her feelings about reading the text while sitting in her car near a police station. She suddenly noticed that policemen seemed suspicious that she was loitering near the station. Her internal alert system exposed my own assumptions of white privilege (namely that I expect to be able to read Scripture wherever and whenever I want). These experiences have convinced me of the importance of taking our Bibles and reading them in a variety of settings.

Of course, to read Scripture outdoors in winter requires its own level of strategies. On some days, I carried a small Psalter with me on my walk and read a few Psalms as I strolled through my neighborhood. On rainy days, I read a couple of Psalms from my sleeping porch. When it turned particularly cold, I read from the warmth of my car. The primary goal was to push myself outside of comfortable indoor settings and to prompt my body to feel the language of the Psalms when surrounded by the beauty and the elements of the nature. To read about the trees rejoicing (Psalm 96:12) when standing beneath trees or walking past them evokes a different feeling than one experiences while sitting in one's study. At stake, in this hermeneutical experiment is discovering the possibility that the text draws its life from the reality of the world and does not simply represent an idea of the world that points us toward spiritual truths. The danger of treating the images in texts as metaphors to deeper insights has become so common that many of us assume it as normative. Far too often the Jordan River is not so much about an actual body of water, but is about a spiritual kind of cleansing that comes as we look beyond our finite bodies to perceive the deeper meaning of a text that only enlightened minds can grasp. This form of gnosticism has so infiltrated much of western Christianity that even our understandings of salvation primarily relate to our souls rather than to our bodies (and often has more to do with theories of life after death rather than with the reality of our daily existence). Reading Scripture outdoors represents a small counter-cultural step in a theological attempt to re-establish the place of our bodies and the world around us as essential elements of a truly incarnational theology.

Both the structure and the contents of the book of Psalms provide clues that can guide us on a journey towards integrating the experiences and insights we discover. In his book *The Green Psalter*, Arthur Walker-Jones describes the book of Psalms as a guide to ways of inhabiting the world. Walker-Jones develops this approach to the Psalms around the widely accepted understanding that the book of Psalms is a collection of five books intended to provide a parallel to the five books of the *Torah* (sometimes referred to as the five books of Moses: Genesis, Exodus, Leviticus, Numbers, and Deuteronomy).[1] The Psalms then present the wisdom and teachings of David in a way that is parallel to how the *Torah* presents the teachings of Moses. For Walker-Jones, this insight includes the importance of recognizing the central role of Earth throughout these texts. The opening scenes in Genesis with its creation narratives provides a rich backdrop to the opening of the book of Psalms with its twin emphasis on the role of *Torah* and the images of creation. In Psalm 1, those who are happy (flourish) are the ones who delight in the law of the LORD and meditate on it around the clock (vs. 2). As a result, they begin to resemble the goodness of creation, like verdant trees rooted by a stream that produce an abundance of fruit and a vast canopy of foliage (vs. 3). It is important to note that this Psalm sets this alongside an alternative image from nature where chaff is blown away by the wind (vs. 4). From the beginning, then, the Psalms depict differentiated experiences of the world as ways to grow in wisdom on our journey through life. Psalm 1 provides a clear

---

[1] Arthur Walker-Jones, *The Green Psalter: Resources for an Ecological Spirituality.* Minneapolis: Fortress Press, 2009, 21.

example of how the Psalter offers us an invitation to grow into its wisdom and teaching.

Not only the language and images of the Psalter, but even the structure of the book of Psalms with its parallels to the *Torah* invite us to find our place on a pilgrimage that runs from creation through exile and liberation that moves toward a promised land flowing with milk and honey. Along the way, we share diverse experiences that include the full range of human emotions that we encounter: from anger and grief to joy and thanksgiving. Within this structure there is movement towards discovering integrative moments. One can see it within individual Psalms where the Psalmist's cries of desolation and anguish shift through the course of the Psalm towards acceptance and praise as the Psalmist recalls God's faithfulness in the past. We can also see it within the contour of the book of Psalms as a whole as it moves towards joining the earth and all of its creatures in praise. Walker-Jones observes that "the creation imagery focuses on the individual, one of several indications that the Psalter is to be read as journey of a person of faith."[2]

This journey is presented as a winding road of exploration by a collection of diverse voices that encourage us to discover the possibility of taking our place within the choir that sings a song of thanksgiving for the gift of life. The Psalms give voice to how we feel along the way by articulating the emotional themes of the Advent season (hope, peace, joy, and love) while also expressing feelings of depression,

---

[2] Walker-Jones, *The Green Psalter*, 29.

melancholy, despair, and loneliness. In these moments, reading the Psalms in the cold and damp provides us with an embodied experience of solidarity even as the Psalmist urges us to experience these moments within the context of God's unfailing mercy.

What prompted this experiment was a discovery that the language and images of the Psalms overlapped with my work on biblical hermeneutics that prioritizes the place of the earth and emphasizes the preferential option for the poor that runs throughout Scripture. This discovery bubbled up during a month long stay at Mepkin Abbey, a Cistercian monastery in South Carolina, as I sang through the Psalter in the daily offices. In the choir stalls alongside the monks, I chanted the Psalms and discovered the ubiquitous use of the language of nature as well as the frequent references to justice for the poor. During my walks across the monastery grounds, I found myself reflecting on the images of the Psalms as I strolled beneath the massive live oaks or as I looked out across the water of the Cooper River.

The process of taking the language of the Psalms into our bodies as we walk through the world opens up a new way of perceiving our relationship to God, nature, and ourselves. To read and recite the Psalms outside is to move beyond our carefully controlled indoor environments and to encounter new possibilities of hearing and responding to these diverse texts. This is particularly true in terms of shifting our relationship to the text from the passive version of listening to others read or chant the text to our own engagement with the text. In fact, I am convinced that the main rationale for the use of the Psalter on Sunday mornings resides in the goal of exposing us to the diverse language and imagery of the Psalter as a resource for us to draw on during our daily lives. Such an understanding of the Psalms aligns with Calvin's goals and practices of singing the Psalms in worship in the hope that we will take these songs (which critics referred to as Genevan jigs) with us during the week. The practice of building a vocabulary from the Psalms supports the aim of growth in Christian piety through the times of joy and pain that are part of all of our lives. The richness of the Psalter with its vast emotional bandwidth that includes lament, anger, joy, grief, and acceptance offers us ways to process our feelings and experiences in conversation with our experience of the divine.

The practice of reading the Psalms outside grows in importance as we recognize ways in which the Psalter itself draws on the natural world as primary material to portray faithful ways to live. In doing so, the Psalms do not avoid the complexity of the world. Instead, the Psalms use both positive and challenging images of nature to prompt us to examine our place in the world created by God. Reading the Psalms outside, then, is not an exercise of so-called natural theology or a romanticization of creation. Instead, it looks to align our experiences with our attempts to see ourselves and our relationship to the world around us. The Psalter offers us an important corrective against our tendencies to look at the world and ourselves through rose-colored lenses. To open our eyes as we walk in the world is to acknowledge both the beauty and suffering of Earth.

Again, it is critical to notice that nature is not simply a metaphor that points to a deeper truth (and can be left behind or forgotten). Instead, nature itself serves as an instructor to us. For example, Psalm 19 provides a potent description of the parallel ways in which creation and *Torah* provide us with moments of encounter with the glory of God. William Brown points to the similarities in the Psalmist's descriptions of the glory of God that is evident in the world around us (vs. 1-6) and that which permeates the teachings of the *Torah* (vs. 7-11). Brown concludes that "creation and *torah* in Psalm 19 are not simply juxtaposed; they are interrelated."[3] To read the Psalms while we sit, stand, or walk through creation then is to open up the possibility of correcting our vision and discovering our place through the divine insights at the intersection of word and world.

A favorite image of John Calvin for Scripture was that of spectacles or lenses that help us see ourselves and the world rightly (as entirely dependent upon God). Calvin's own love of nature as revelatory of God's goodness in creation (a depiction that is often either overlooked or downplayed by many of Calvin's interpreters) points to his own belief and experience that an illumined mind and heart will perceive the beauty and goodness of God in the world around us. Here, I am proposing the outdoor reading of the Psalms as a set of bifocal lenses that provide important corrections to our often faulty sight. Let me be clear, though, that neither the Psalter or Nature offer us rose-colored lenses. Instead, both force us to wrestle with a

---

[3] William P. Brown, "Deep Calls to Deep: The Ecology of Praise in the Psalms" in *The Oxford Handbook of the Bible and Ecology*, eds. Hillary Marlow and Mark Harris (Oxford: Oxford University Press, 2022), 167.

wide range of emotional responses. The book of Psalms provides a wider range of genres including extensive sections of lament; to read the Psalter is to prompt ourselves to come to terms with the sense of sadness, desolation, and loneliness that we experience in life. It is important to notice that this sense of isolation includes a sense of estrangement from God. Psalm 22 captures this emotion with its dramatic outcry: "My God, my God, why have you forsaken me? Why are you so far from saving me, from the words of my groaning? O my God, I cry by day, but you do not answer, and by night, but I find no rest" (vs. 1-2). For Christians, the attribution of this text to Jesus as he dies on the cross reinforces the way in which the Psalms provide us with a vocabulary to express our deepest feelings. For example, when I walk down the street near my house, I encounter various forms of trash that people have thrown out of their car windows. In response, I began what I refer to as a prayer practice of picking up rubbish including beer bottles, old clothes, car parts, letters, and endless amounts of fast-food containers as an act of prayer to help the earth breathe. To pick up trash is not to fix a problem (I quickly discovered that my efforts would never alleviate the constant clutter), but to force myself to acknowledge and respond to the pain that the earth suffers from being smothered by human consumption and neglect.

Wisdom then comes to us in multiple forms. Our encounter with the beauty of nature is certainly one prominent form, but we experience Earth in moments of grandeur as well as in forms of suffering and death. From the roadkill of carcasses that litter our highways to the clearcut hillsides where forests have been ravaged to provide us with building materials, opening our eyes to the world around us presents us with vastly different experiences that engage and provoke visceral reactions in our bodies.

Word and world both present forms of truth-telling that place us in moments of decision. These *kerygmatic* (gospel) moments require a response from us. Will we close the book of Psalms when it does not provide us with the comfort or insight that we crave? Will we turn our eyes away from the pain and suffering of the natural world and place the blame on someone else? Or do these moments of encounter actually offer us the form of revelation that we most desperately need?

The Soundtrack of the Psalms

There is another way to explore points of synchronicity between the wisdom of the word and the world. I decided to start listening to various recordings of the Psalms on my neighborhood walks. I started by searching for oral recordings of the Psalter that I could access on my iPhone. There is a myriad of options on YouTube and other platforms. While the choice may correlate to personal preference, there are certain interesting distinctions to note as it relates to our primary interest in attuning to Earth imagery in the Psalms. Listening to the Psalms allows one to correlate the bodily experience of walking through woods and neighborhoods with the acoustic text of the Psalter in one's ears. Here the sounds of birdcalls pierce the technological production of the recordings (a kind of dual soundtrack in which Nature is pushed to the background in order for the reading of Scripture to be primary in our hearing).

The recording of Psalms 1-41 (often identified by scholars as the first book of Psalms) by Melody Joy (Williams), who is a contemporary Christian recording artist, offer a distinctive interpretation. She reads straight through the chapters of the Psalms without any demarcation between the Psalms. Her melodic reading is accompanied by a background soundscape ("soaking music") all of which makes for an ethereal experience largely devoid of highlighting Earth images in the Psalms and instead focused on a reading of the Psalms that highlights an introspective dialogue between Yahweh and the self. In contrast, the recording of the Coverdale version of the Psalter by Paul Edmonson announces each Psalm while the reading provides a particular shape to each Psalm that highlights the inherent contrasts and emotional resolutions that are typical of the Psalter (e.g., the movement from lament to thanksgiving). I found that one of the advantages to listening repeatedly to the Psalter was the way that it increased my fluency, memory, and appreciation of the Psalms.

An alternative approach is to listen to chanted or sung versions of the Psalms outside. The myriad of available options can be broadly grouped in different categories. I started by listening to English language chant settings of the Psalms. Like the spoken versions of the Psalms, the choice of translation immediately provides an interpretive lens. This is highlighted by both the chant tone and the performance of the recording. I found fewer collections of chanted Psalms and more recordings of individual Psalms. This led to a choice of listening to one Psalm on repeat on longer walks. An advantage of this approach is that my attention to the music began to shift towards a secondary or subconscious element of the Psalm and allowed me to keep a focus on the world around me while looking for intersections between my bodily experience and the soundtrack of the Psalms. As I learned these sung settings of the Psalms, my experience became more participatory and integrative in discerning connections between Word and World.

I also listened to recordings of the Psalms in different languages and following different chant tones. This variety provides for rich alternatives that can broaden our interactions with the Psalter. I became particularly fond of the choral group Harpa Dei whose extensive recordings provide options that highlight all of these approaches. For those who prefer newer sung settings of the Psalms there are extensive recordings that range from Anglican hymnody to contemporary Christian songs. One interesting sidelight is that many of the you tube videos that accompany these recordings include nature scenes and outdoor settings. The pervasive nature of the images of creation throughout the Psalms has prompted others to look for these connections.

A more traditional approach towards praying the Psalms is integral to daily prayer. My own experience of chanting the Psalms alongside the monks of Mepkin Abbey led me to more deeply explore the significance of their role in Christian formation and spirituality. At Mepkin, the monks observe the seven offices of the day by focusing their prayer lives around the Psalter which they sing through every two weeks. The history of associating particular Psalms with times/offices of the day is an important component to their arrangement of the Psalter. While the rhythms of monastic life place an emphasis on interiority rather than drawing primary attention to the Earth that is replete throughout the Psalter, monks spend so much time with the Psalms each day in prayer that the Psalter becomes deeply internalized. Since monasteries are often in bucolic settings, monks develop the capacity to transfer their familiarity with the Psalter to the beauty of the earth that surrounds them. For example, at Mepkin Abbey the majestic presence of the live oak trees draped with Spanish moss alongside the Cooper River provide a breathtaking portrait of Psalmist's reference to trees planted by the water.

Curating the Psalms

There are different ways to think about using collections of Psalms as interpretive resources for our experiences in the world. I will highlight a few options that are helpful in drawing on the rich images of the Psalter. First, one can simply follow the built-in structure of the Psalter itself by working through the five books of the Psalms. A particularly ambitious schedule is proposed by Victor in *The Watcher's Psalter* where one is encouraged to read each section of the Psalter on weekdays followed by the entire Psalter on weekends:

Monday: Psalms 1-41 (Book One)

Tuesday: Psalms 42-72 (Book Two)

Wednesday: Psalms 73-89 (Book Three)

Thursday: Psalms 90-106 (Book Four)

Friday: Psalms 107-150 (Book Five)

Saturday and Sunday: Psalms 1-150.[4]

I would note that Book Five pays increased attention to the role of Earth and the way in which we as humans are invited to join in a chorus of praise with all creation. Highlighting Book Five of the Psalms offers us significant resources that encourage us to re-orient ourselves to Earth and find our place alongside the rest of Nature as in joins in its praise of God.

A second possibility is to construct a collection of Psalms for a particular walk. In this approach, the geographical features and topography of the land would provide a guide for selecting specific Psalms to group together on a walk. For example, a river walk would draw on water images in the Psalms, a mountain hike would draw from Psalms with images of hills, mountains, and rocks, a forest walk would select Psalms that highlight trees. An index could be added with references to the variety of animals throughout the Psalms so that they would be available as particular species

---

[4] https://docs.google.com/document/d/1UiEvvslgFu-Z2Kl6IdGneXgG2J0E4dBskD_BBdUDRHc/edit

are seen. Here, nature provides a guide to our reading of the Psalms.

A third approach would be to create a more permanent walk that draws on the images of particular Psalms. I am calling this approach Stations of the Psalter. It adapts the concept of the stations of the cross with specific prayers at stops along a journey. This would be a great project for a walking path for a congregation that has enough property to support it. The traditional number of 14 stations of cross could be used to encourage the reading of 14 Psalms (or selections from Psalms) that are coordinated with the local landscape. A walk through a congregational garden can include Psalms with reference to plants, trees, flowers, and food. A walk that includes the sanctuary can draw on the Psalm's references to the temple as God's dwelling place. The walk could make primary use of handouts that show a map of numbered locations with a brief Psalm text to read at each station/stop. For congregations with resources and connections, local artists could create pieces for each of the stations and a relevant Psalm text could be referenced so that individuals could look up the text to read it (from a Bible or on their smart phone).

Finally, a related idea would be to create a walk that draws on other prominent themes in the Psalter. For example, the devotional readings in this book highlighted the traditional advent themes of hope, peace, love, and joy. The Psalms are rich in their use of emotional language that ranges from lament and anger to comfort and delight. The Psalms' own movement between diverse emotional feelings (often within a single Psalm) provides an important tutorial for us to express ourselves. Modeling this by showing the movement with the Psalms themselves provides a critical resource for people in expressing the full range of their emotions withing the context of a prayer walk.

One other important note is to acknowledge the central role of the poor throughout the Psalter. In a recent reflection on reading Scripture, I have highlighted two key theological issues that are grounded in Scripture and respond to the needs of our time: 1) the centrality of the earth in the witness of Scripture; and 2) Scripture's commitment to the preferential option of the poor.[5] While we have explored options for linking the reading of the Psalms with greater attention to Earth, it is also critical for us to recover the sustained attention with the Psalter on the significance of caring for the poor. We must avoid the danger of using Scripture to pacify our own interests and to appease our desire for aesthetic pleasure which is a particular risk of mining the Psalms for lovely nature images as we walk through our cultivated and protected gardens and landscape. Hence, a Psalter walk that acknowledges and wrestles with the painful conditions of those trapped in poverty offers an essential correction by naming and confronting these issues in our neighborhoods. As the Psalmist helps us give voice to the needs of the poor, we will find ourselves called to

---

[5] Paul Galbreath, *Word and Sacrament: Tracing the Theological Movements of Reformed Worship* (Louisville: Westminster/John Knox Press, 2024). See Chapter 7 on Scriptural interpretation. See also the classic work from Leonardo Boff, *Cry of the Earth, Cry of the Poor*, trans. Phillip Berryman (Maryknoll, NY: Orbis Books, 2002).

participate in caring for our neighbors and our community. Food pantries, prisons, community centers, health services (particularly that focus on caring for the poor) are sites that can be coordinated with Psalm texts as a call to remember and act so that we may join with the divine impulse to care for our neighbors in need. One way to facilitate this exercise is by creating a walking/driving map that takes us to places that provide essential services for those who are poor. The map could include a Psalm selection and a prayer to read at each location so that over time as we begin to pay closer attention to the places and the people who come to them that we find ourselves aware of and engaged in the work and ministry that occurs there.

The goal then is to allow the Psalms to change our lives by opening our eyes to the beauty and the suffering that surrounds us. When we only read the Bible inside the walls of our church or as private devotionals inside our homes, we run the risk of taming and limiting the powerful language and imagery of Scripture. Taking the Psalms outside is a small and important step in hearing, seeing, and connecting the Psalter with the world around us.

Bundling Hope

A Sermon on Psalm 71:1-18

Last year, I retired from teaching theology at Union Presbyterian Seminary. I decided to mark the occasion in an unusual way by spending the month of July at Mepkin Abbey in South Carolina. It's a Trappist monastery that is located on the banks of the Cooper River outside of Charleston on what was one of the oldest plantations of English settlers in the U.S. Once a year the monastery offers a program that invites participants to come and live like a monk by dedicating each day to pray and work (*ora et labora*). You might wonder why I decided to get up at 3:30 each morning to join in the seven times of prayer each day; Or what caused me to welcome my janitorial assignment to help clean the eldercare facilities? Why would a recently retired Reformed theologian run away to a Roman Catholic monastery for a month?

I would like to believe that God was involved in it; that it was an act of providence. A couple of my students at Union Seminary told me about Mepkin Abbey – and described it as a holy place – one of those thin places where heaven and earth seem to come together. From the moment that I drove through the Abbey gates and found myself underneath the giant live oak trees covered with Spanish moss, I felt the Spirit's presence. As a Trappist monastery, Mepkin Abbey is a place of silence where few words are spoken in order to allow each person to focus on their commitment to grow in Christian faith. For me, it was also a bewildering place. Trying to navigate six different prayer books while singing and praying with the monks in the choir stalls offers its own unique challenge. Or hoping to guess what is in the unmarked bottles on the meal counters comes with its own risk – one of my colleagues who thought he was adding honey to his peanut butter sandwich ended up with a surprise hot sauce sandwich.

In spite of these challenges, the highlight of my stay there was the opportunity to chant the Psalms with the monks. I began each day by making my way to the church for the Vigils service at 4 a.m. At Vigils, we sang a minimum of eight Psalms each morning and over the course of all of the services each day, I sang up to twenty Psalms a day. During the month, the Psalms began to work their way into my mind and body. When I was sweeping the halls or moving mattresses, I found myself humming a Psalm that we sang earlier that day.

Ironically, this is exactly what John Calvin, the father of Presbyterianism, had in mind when he reformed the church in Geneva over five hundred years ago. Calvin believed that a commitment to singing the Psalms was central in encouraging Christians to grow in their piety. To facilitate this goal, Calvin wrote and collected new versions of the Psalms for the congregation to sing in worship. At the time, critics of Calvin found this practice so controversial that they accused Calvin and his followers of singing Genevan jigs – which sounds to me like a crazy 16th century version of praise music. For Calvin, the goal of regularly singing the Psalms was to get Scripture into our minds, hearts, and bodies – so that we find ourselves on Tuesday morning humming one of the Psalms that we sang in church on Sunday. Calvin once described the book of Psalms as "an anatomy of the soul; for there is not an emotion of which anyone can be conscious that is not represented as in a mirror." To make this point another way: Whatever we feel and whatever emotions we experience – joy, anger, or despair; we can find them described in the book of Psalms.

This range of human feeling is what led Calvin to make the Psalms the primary hymnody for the congregation. He believed that whenever we see ourselves in light of the contours of Scripture, we are greatly helped in our search for God. I remember teaching a Sunday school class on Presbyterian worship in a small congregation that I served many years ago in Oregon. One Sunday morning an older woman brought a copy of the hymnal that she used when she was a child; it consisted almost entirely of settings of the Psalms. For centuries, the singing of the Psalms was a regular part of Sunday worship. It is only in our life-time that we have wandered off in new directions seeking to find new songs that will bring us new life.

My time at Mepkin renewed in me this commitment to the Psalms. It has inspired my current writing project of a daily devotional book for Advent based on the Psalms. This morning, I'd like for us to explore Psalm 71. The Psalmist invites us to take inventory of our lives in order to recognize God's faithful presence that sustains us each step along the way. In Psalm 71, these memories are bracketed by hope: "You, O Lord, are my hope, my trust, O Lord, from my youth." The Psalmist looks back over his life and recognizes that God's presence has accompanied him from the time of his birth. This practice of reflecting on one's life in order to discern and discover the presence of God offers us a kind of autobiographical spiritual exercise. Where in your life did you sense God's presence that has accompanied you? What times in your life can you remember that provides a basis for hope? Notice that the Psalmist adopts this practice not to avoid or deny his feelings of vulnerability, but in order to address them. To remember God's past presence provides a source for hope especially in facing difficult times. When attacked by enemies and surrounded by those who try to disparage and harm him, the Psalmist remains steadfast in his conviction that God will accompany him in times of trouble: "I will hope continually and will praise you yet more and more."

The Psalmist reminds us of an essential element of faith: *Hope grows in the soil of memory.* Looking back over his life, he remembers moments when God's presence sustained him. Even as he faces new challenges, he draws hope from God's faithfulness that accompanied him through both good and difficult times of life.

So how can this Psalm serve as a source of inspiration for us? Let me be clear that there is a risk in reading this Psalm as providing a word of individual encouragement to each of us. Psalm 71 is not about the power of positive thinking or a form of self-help therapy. Instead, it is critical for us to remember the role this Psalm played in the lives of those who gathered for worship long ago. This Psalm functions as a collective song – a reminder of the significance of encouraging each other to bundle our memories of the places where we have experienced God's presence in our lives.

This morning, I am inviting us to try out a practice of sharing our hope with one another. What might it look like for us to gather up our hopes and offer them as a resource to help us move forward? How can we encourage one another by sharing our memories of God's presence in our lives and creating an oasis where hope can sustain us through the difficulties that life will inevitably come our way? Only by drawing on the resources of our shared memory – the witness of Scripture and the testimonies of our lives will we discover the strength to endure. That is why at the conclusion of the sermon, you will be invited to write a word or a sentence on a card that points to a place and moment in your life when you experienced God's presence. We will collect these cards during the offering and have them on a bulletin board and table in the narthex for you to see after the service. Together, we will be creating our own Psalm of God's faithful presence in our lives.

Where is it that you experienced God's presence? Let me share with you a recent moment from my life. Last month, Jan and I took a trip to Santa Fe to visit friends. One of our favorite places north of Santa Fe is a sacred site called Chimayo. There, a church was built over an ancient healing site. Adjacent to the sanctuary is a small chapel off to the side with a little room that has a hole in the ground. One or two people at a time can enter into this tiny room where you can dig up a scoop of the holy dirt that has produced countless miracles over the years. The walls of the chapel are lined with crutches that are no longer needed and with pictures of those who have experienced healing during their visit to Chimayo.

No matter how you may feel about the idea of holy dirt (and count me among the skeptics) the power of the space is undeniable. Chimayo represents an oasis of shared hope in the midst of a region that struggles with poverty and racial discrimination against indigenous and Hispanic people. In this small chapel, though, an aura of hope extends equally to all who are open to receive it. Whoever comes with a need for healing is welcome to kneel and scoop up some dirt and receive the spirit of hope that permeates the walls of this modest stucco chapel. Within the walls of this small church, the memory of God's healing presence is proclaimed. The words of the Psalmist come to life: "O God, do not be far from me; O my God, make haste to help me." "My mouth will tell of your righteous acts, of your deeds of salvation all day long."

Friends, how will these words of the Psalmist take root in our lives? What memories of God's presence can we share with one another that will strengthen our faith? How can this church community, called New Hope, inspire us to continually declare our praise of God? As we share memories of God's presence in our lives, the Spirit strengthens us to live into the Psalmist's depiction of faithful living where hope and praise become continual in our lives. As we draw on the Spirit's presence in one another's life, we lean into the vision that the Apostle Paul describes in our reading from Romans – to experience God's steadfastness and encouragement that allows us to live in harmony with one another. When we create a collective Psalm of the places where we have encountered God's presence, we draw strength from one another for the journey ahead. As we prepare to share a memory of God's presence in our lives, receive this blessing from our reading from Romans: "May the God of hope fill you will all joy and peace in believing, so that you abound in hope by the power of the Holy Spirit." Amen.

Where and when have you experienced God's presence in your life. Write down a memory of one of those times:

Afterword

Cláudio Carvalhaes

I remember when Paul told me about his decision to go to Mepkin Abbey in South Carolina. He was retiring from his tenured position at Union Presbyterian Seminary after eighteen years of teaching in the fields of Worship and Theology. In some ways Paul was facing a huge rite of passage, leaving a job to which he devoted his whole life with so much love, and now beginning a new chapter of his life with different purposes and forms of meaning. During the time he was at the Abbey, he sent me a couple of emails describing the surprises, difficulties, and wonders of the challenges of living together in such a beautiful place. He would tell me about the amazing walk he took from his room to the chapel under the moon and deep in the darkness for the first office/service at 4 a.m. each morning. He was a full participant in the daily chores, lectures, and life of the Abbey. But what stood out for him the most during that time was the singing of the Psalms. During his stay there he read the whole book of Psalms twice, reading it every day. That experience marked Paul's life so deeply that he began exploring the Psalms and read them again closely, now writing meditations on many of them.

This book is the result of that deep experience with himself, with the Monks, with the land, and with God. I am grateful Paul wanted to offer these reflections in the format and in the context of the liturgical time of the Advent, both correcting some of the ways Christians read the Psalms and expanding the understanding of Advent itself. While many years ago, Paul turned his heart and mind and body to the earth; everything he does now has a deep relationship with the earth. That is why the earth is everywhere in this book and why he asks us to read the Psalms outside of our homes and buildings. With that form of reading the Psalms, he helps us engage our own feelings with the vastness of emotions seen in the Psalm in order to learn how we can mirror, relate, and engage with the feelings we feel when looking at the mountains and the sky, touching the earth, and paying attention to God's grace everywhere around us. Paired with his devotional book *Elemental: A Journey through Lent with the Earth*, this book offers a vivid re-orientation through these two important liturgical seasons of the Christian calendar from the perspective of God's creation.

I have known Paul Galbreath for over two decades now and Paul is both the same and a very different person from when I first met him. His passion for the word of God is still vivid! I remember my first encounters with him when he lived in Louisville leading the office of worship of the Presbyterian Church, U.S.A. One night at his house he was passionately asking how scripture could speak to people if spoken outside of the church buildings. This book seems to be a response and a closure to that question. Yes, he got it! And in much richer ways, he is offering us a path to hear the word of God in ancient and fresh ways. As a seasoned theologian, Paul has expanded the Reformed faith in beautiful and nuanced ways through his many books. But it is in his Lent and Advent books that he takes us to the very basic gestures of our faith.

With both books, Paul leads us to rediscover the richness of an ancient faith made anew, showing us the power of Scripture to respond to the disasters of our time while giving us the heart we need to face this very difficult time in which we are living. Each book Paul writes is a mirror of himself, of someone who knows how to listen deeply to God, to people, and to the land, and from that listening, he comes out offering us a way of being in the world. I have been so blessed to have journeyed with Paul through these years. It is in Lent and now through Advent that I feel the gentleness, the blessings, the power, and the wisdom of his liturgical writings. I pray you will feel that too. What a precious book this is!